PRINCEWILL LAGANG

Russia: The Second World's Most Dominant Military: The Anatomy of Power

Contents

1

Introduction

This book offers an in-depth exploration of Russia's military prowess, shedding light on the factors that make it a global powerhouse. While Russia's size alone often grabs attention, its true military strength lies in a combination of historical context, technological advancement, and strategic planning. The narrative goes beyond surface-level assumptions, diving into how Russia has carefully shaped its military forces over the decades. From its Soviet roots to the modern-day, the book reveals the decisions that have defined Russia's defense capabilities.

At the heart of this power is a strategic understanding of global politics, where Russia's military positioning plays a crucial role in shaping its foreign policy. The book highlights Russia's approach to maintaining a balance of power on the world stage, examining how it leverages its military to influence international relations. This includes the use of diplomacy, cyber warfare, and traditional military force to assert dominance. It also reveals the underlying tactics and decision-making processes that allow Russia to navigate an ever-changing geopolitical landscape.

Lastly, the book takes the reader behind the scenes of Russia's military infrastructure. It explores the cutting-edge technologies and innovations that power its defense sector, from advanced weaponry to military logistics. The book provides a glimpse into the complex network of people, systems, and technologies that work in tandem to ensure Russia's military might. Through this lens, readers will gain a comprehensive understanding of Russia's strategic military posture and the ways in which it continues to shape global security.

2

Strategic Geography and Defense

C hapter 1:

Russia's sheer size and geographical diversity present both significant challenges and advantages in shaping its defense strategy. The country spans across two continents, Europe and Asia, with vast stretches of land, from dense forests and expansive plains to mountainous terrains and frigid arctic regions. This wide variety in geography has forced Russia to adapt its military strategies, taking into account the environmental obstacles and opportunities each region presents. In the western part of the country, Russia faces proximity to NATO countries, which requires a defense focus on maintaining a strong presence in Europe. To the east, vast distances between key cities and limited infrastructure make quick mobilization difficult, necessitating a defense strategy that emphasizes deterrence and the strategic placement of resources.

The Russian military must also contend with the challenges posed by its harsh winters and varying climates, requiring equipment and strategies tailored to survive and thrive in extreme conditions. This includes specialized training for troops to operate in environments ranging from the icy tundra to the dense forests. The vast Siberian region, which holds a significant portion of Russia's natural resources, also needs defense strategies that protect these valuable assets. This often involves securing critical supply lines, ensuring military readiness, and using the land's natural barriers as tactical advantages in case of potential invasions. Thus, Russia's strategic geography dictates not only the positioning of its forces but also the innovation of specific tactics suited to these varying terrains.

Additionally, Russia's defense strategies are influenced by historical experiences, particularly the invasions that have historically threatened its security. The expansive landmass offers both natural defenses and challenges; for instance, the expansive space between Russia's borders and major cities makes it difficult for enemies to penetrate, but it also means that the Russian military must spread its resources thin across the vast territory. This has led Russia to invest in an array of defensive measures, from anti-air systems to advanced missile technology, ensuring that its expansive borders remain under constant protection.

The Nuclear Arsenal: A Deterrent Force

Chapter 2:

Russia's nuclear arsenal has long been a cornerstone of its defense strategy, acting as a powerful deterrent to potential threats. As one of the world's largest nuclear powers, Russia's nuclear weapons serve as a key element in maintaining national security and asserting its global influence. The strategic importance of these weapons is reflected in the doctrine that Russia has developed over decades, emphasizing the role of nuclear capabilities in deterring aggression and ensuring survival against superior conventional forces. Unlike many Western nations, Russia continues to invest heavily in its nuclear arsenal, ensuring that it remains a formidable force on the world stage.

The presence of an extensive nuclear stockpile allows Russia to maintain a form of "mutually assured destruction" (MAD) with other nuclear powers, which contributes to a delicate balance of power. Russia's arsenal includes both intercontinental ballistic missiles (ICBMs) and submarine-launched ballistic missiles (SLBMs), which can strike targets anywhere in the world. Furthermore, Russia's focus on developing hypersonic missiles has ensured that its nuclear deterrent remains technologically competitive. These advances in missile technology allow Russia to circumvent traditional missile defense systems, increasing the credibility of its nuclear deterrence strategy. By investing in these advanced technologies, Russia maintains the strategic advantage in an age where technological superiority is key to global security.

The geopolitical role of Russia's nuclear arsenal also extends beyond deterrence, as it allows the country to influence international negotiations and strategic alignments. Russia's nuclear capabilities often play a central role in its foreign policy and negotiations, allowing the country to secure its interests on the global stage. In the context of arms control, Russia has been involved in several key treaties, such as the New START Treaty, aimed at limiting nuclear arms proliferation. These treaties not only serve to reduce the risk of nuclear conflict but also highlight the centrality of nuclear weapons in shaping the security landscape, with Russia maintaining a position of strength due to its substantial nuclear stockpile.

The Role of Technology in Modern Warfare

C hapter 3:

Technology plays an increasingly pivotal role in shaping the nature of modern warfare, and Russia has made significant strides in harnessing technological advancements to enhance its military capabilities. One of the most significant areas of focus has been cyber warfare. As global interconnectivity increases, the ability to disrupt enemy communications, power grids, and infrastructure becomes a critical component of military strategy. Russia has been accused of employing cyber-attacks as part of its broader geopolitical strategy, engaging in digital warfare to influence political outcomes and disrupt adversaries without direct confrontation. The growing importance of cyber defense has pushed Russia to develop sophisticated countermeasures, establishing a new frontier in warfare where the battlefield is no longer confined to physical space.

In addition to cyber capabilities, artificial intelligence (AI) and machine learning are transforming military operations. Russia has invested in developing autonomous systems, such as drones and unmanned vehicles, that can operate in hostile environments without risking human lives. These AI-driven systems allow for increased precision in targeting and a more efficient allocation of resources, thus enhancing Russia's military readiness. The use of AI also extends to enhancing intelligence-gathering capabilities, where algorithms can process vast amounts of data to identify patterns and predict enemy movements, providing a strategic advantage. However, the integration of such technology also raises concerns about the potential for unintended consequences, such as the autonomous use of force without human oversight.

Another key advancement in Russia's military technology is the development of precision-guided weaponry. These advanced munitions offer unparalleled accuracy, allowing for the targeting of specific military assets with minimal collateral damage. Such precision is particularly advantageous in conflict zones where the protection of civilian infrastructure is crucial. Russia's investment in missile systems, such as the Iskander and the S-400, has made it a formidable force in terms of striking targets with pinpoint accuracy, ensuring that it can assert power with reduced risk of escalation. By embracing these technologies, Russia aims to maintain technological parity with NATO and other military powers, positioning itself as a modern and adaptable force in the evolving landscape of global warfare.

5

The Russian Air Force: Aerial Dominance

C hapter 4:

The Russian Air Force has undergone significant evolution, reflecting the changing dynamics of modern warfare and Russia's need to maintain air superiority in both regional and global conflicts. Initially built to counter NATO's air forces during the Cold War, the Russian Air Force now incorporates a diverse array of advanced fighter jets, bombers, and surveillance aircraft. These aircraft are designed not only for air-to-air combat but also for strategic bombing, reconnaissance, and support for ground forces. The focus on multi-role fighters like the Su-27 and Su-57 highlights Russia's emphasis on versatility, ensuring that its air force can adapt to various operational needs across different theaters of conflict.

Russia's aerial dominance also relies heavily on its advanced air defense systems. The S-400 system, for example, is regarded as one of the most formidable anti-aircraft missile systems in the world. These systems provide protection against a wide range of aerial threats, from conventional fighter jets to advanced stealth aircraft, and ensure that Russian airspace remains secure. The integration of these defense systems with other military branches allows Russia to maintain a layered defense, creating a comprehensive air protection strategy. By securing air superiority through both offensive and defensive measures, Russia aims to control key regions, limit the effectiveness of enemy air forces, and maintain a strategic advantage in conflicts.

The role of the Russian Air Force is not limited to territorial defense. In modern conflicts, air power has proven crucial for both offensive operations and deterrence. Russia's ability to project air power beyond its borders has been evident in recent military interventions, such as in Syria, where Russian aircraft conducted bombing campaigns to support allied forces. These operations showcase the Russian Air Force's capabilities in carrying out complex, long-range missions. Moreover, the integration of cutting-edge technologies, such as precision-guided munitions and drone warfare, allows the Russian Air Force to enhance its operational effectiveness. The continual modernization of its fleet ensures that Russia's air power remains a significant element in its military strategy, providing both deterrence and combat effectiveness in contemporary conflicts.

6

The Navy's Global Presence

C **hapter 5:**

This chapter delves into Russia's naval capabilities, focusing on its extensive fleet and the strategic use of submarines. The Russian Navy has long been a symbol of power and global reach, with a particular emphasis on its nuclear-powered submarines. These vessels are designed for both deterrence and combat, giving Russia an edge in terms of stealth and firepower beneath the ocean. The chapter explores how Russia maintains a significant presence in key maritime regions, with strategic deployments in the Arctic, Baltic, and Pacific Oceans. The country's icebreaker fleet, in particular, plays a vital role in the Arctic region, asserting Russia's dominance in this increasingly contested area.

Furthermore, the chapter highlights Russia's Arctic strategy, which is driven by a desire to control crucial shipping routes and access natural resources. The Russian Navy's ability to project power across the globe is enhanced by its focus on versatile platforms that can operate in both ice-laden waters and warmer seas. This strategic deployment underscores Russia's growing interest in the Arctic as a geopolitical asset and its efforts to fortify its positions through military and naval dominance. Russia's investments in new-generation submarines capable of carrying nuclear weapons also play a key role in strengthening its deterrent posture and ensuring it remains a formidable naval power.

Finally, the chapter addresses the broader implications of Russia's naval capabilities in the context of international security. With its vast network of ports and access to critical maritime choke points, Russia's global presence can disrupt key shipping lanes and challenge the influence of rival powers. By bolstering its naval forces, Russia continues to maintain a competitive advantage on the world stage, positioning itself as a power capable of influencing global maritime trade and security. The Navy's global presence, then, is not just about hardware, but about maintaining strategic leverage in a rapidly changing geopolitical environment.

7

Land Forces and Armored Strength

C hapter 6:

In this chapter, the focus shifts to Russia's formidable ground forces, examining its tanks, mechanized infantry, and overall military strategy on land. Russia is renowned for its armored strength, with tanks like the T-14 Armata representing the pinnacle of military engineering. These tanks combine advanced technologies in armor, firepower, and mobility, making them a critical asset in modern warfare. The chapter details how Russia's ground forces continue to evolve in response to changing military doctrines, blending traditional armored warfare with new tactics aimed at outmaneuvering opponents. Russian land forces have historically been designed to assert control over vast territories, and this chapter highlights how this legacy shapes current military operations.

The mechanized infantry plays a crucial role in complementing the armored divisions, providing infantry support while maintaining high mobility. The Russian strategy integrates both tanks and infantry in a combined arms approach, enabling coordinated assaults that overwhelm enemy defenses. The chapter also explores how the Russian military has prioritized modernization, investing in new systems to ensure that its land forces remain competitive. Russia's focus on enhancing its artillery, air-defense systems, and electronic warfare capabilities are all part of a broader strategy to enhance the lethality of its ground forces, making them not only powerful but highly adaptable in diverse combat scenarios.

The strategic importance of these land forces cannot be overstated. Whether in regional conflicts or larger scale confrontations, Russia's ability to rapidly deploy and sustain large armored formations offers it significant leverage on the battlefield. This chapter concludes by examining how Russia's military doctrine has placed a premium on fast, decisive ground campaigns, often relying on overwhelming force and the ability to conduct swift operations across vast geographical expanses. In this sense, the Russian army is designed not only to defend the homeland but to project power and influence across borders.

8

The Space Frontier: Military Satellites and Beyond

C hapter 7:

This chapter explores Russia's advancements in space technology, particularly its military applications. Russia has long been a key player in space exploration, and its military use of satellites is one of the most significant aspects of its modern strategy. The Russian military employs a range of satellites for intelligence, surveillance, reconnaissance, and communication purposes, giving it an edge in both conventional and cyber warfare. The chapter highlights Russia's efforts to develop next-generation space technologies, including anti-satellite capabilities, which are designed to neutralize enemy space assets and prevent adversaries from gaining an upper hand in space-based operations.

The chapter also discusses Russia's broader vision for military space exploration, emphasizing the role of space as a critical domain for future warfare. Russia's space program is not only about enhancing its own military capabilities but also about challenging the dominance of other global powers, particularly the United States. The creation of space weapons, along with Russia's partnerships with other nations in space exploration, reflects a desire to control the space frontier and counter potential threats in this strategic domain. These advancements demonstrate how Russia is positioning itself to ensure that it can operate freely in space while simultaneously denying that same capability to its adversaries.

Furthermore, the chapter touches on the broader implications of Russia's military space capabilities for global security. As space becomes an increasingly contested domain, the ability to control and disrupt space-based infrastructure is of immense strategic value. Russia's investments in military satellites and space defense systems indicate its recognition of space as a vital theater for modern warfare. The chapter concludes by exploring the potential future of military space technologies, emphasizing the importance of this domain for Russia's long-term defense strategy.

9

Special Forces and Elite Units

C hapter 8:

In the final chapter, the focus shifts to Russia's special forces and
elite military units, which are often seen as the spearhead of the
country's military operations. Russian special forces, such as the Spetsnaz,
are renowned for their rigorous training, specialized tactics, and ability to
operate in the most challenging environments. The chapter explores the
unique selection and training processes that produce some of the world's most
capable soldiers, focusing on their skills in reconnaissance, sabotage, counter-
terrorism, and direct action missions. These elite units are often deployed in
high-stakes situations, requiring not only advanced combat abilities but also
the capacity to navigate complex geopolitical situations.

The chapter also highlights the global operations of these elite units, which have been involved in various covert actions and operations across the world. Whether it's supporting pro-Russian insurgents or conducting direct strikes against high-value targets, Russia's special forces are strategically positioned to project power and influence beyond its borders. The chapter examines some of the most high-profile operations conducted by Russian special forces, shedding light on their effectiveness and the role they play in Russia's broader foreign policy strategy. These units are seen as instruments of political and military leverage, able to operate independently or in conjunction with other military branches.

Finally, the chapter explores the evolving nature of Russia's special forces in the context of modern warfare. With the rise of hybrid threats and unconventional conflicts, these units are increasingly called upon to deal with irregular warfare and asymmetric threats. The Russian military's emphasis on developing elite units that can swiftly adapt to various challenges reflects a broader trend in global military strategy. The chapter concludes by examining how these units continue to evolve and how their role within the Russian military structure remains crucial to achieving success in both conventional and unconventional operations.

10

Alliances and Proxy Wars

C hapter 9:

This chapter delves into Russia's diplomatic and military strategies through alliances and its involvement in proxy wars. Russia, under Vladimir Putin, has strategically forged alliances with countries that align with its geopolitical goals, particularly in the Middle East and Eastern Europe. The chapter highlights Russia's longstanding partnership with Syria, where it has cemented a military presence to assert its influence in the region. Additionally, the chapter explores Russia's ties with Iran and how these partnerships enable it to project power beyond its borders, especially as it seeks to challenge the West's dominance in global affairs. These alliances also serve as vital tools for Russia to counter NATO and U.S. influence, thus shaping the geopolitical landscape.

Furthermore, the text explores Russia's role in various proxy wars, where it has provided support to insurgent groups or factions opposing Western-backed governments. In Ukraine, Russia's involvement in the ongoing conflict since 2014 has highlighted its strategy of leveraging local conflicts to gain territorial advantage and destabilize neighboring regions. This strategy allows Russia to challenge Western influence without directly engaging in full-scale wars, relying instead on local militias, economic aid, and covert operations. The chapter examines the practical implications of these proxy wars, including the long-term costs and risks for Russia as it faces global condemnation and potential isolation.

The final part of the chapter discusses how these proxy conflicts impact global security. Russia's ability to orchestrate or support proxy wars has made it a central player in modern international relations. While these conflicts may seem distant, they have far-reaching consequences for global peace and stability. From the war in Syria to its actions in Africa, Russia's strategic influence over proxy wars underscores its ambition to reassert itself as a dominant world power, challenging established powers like the United States and its allies. The chapter concludes by reflecting on the lasting effects of these conflicts and the role alliances will continue to play in shaping future global power dynamics.

11

Defense Spending and Economic Priorities

C hapter 10:

In this chapter, the author examines how Russia manages its defense budget amidst the constraints of a strained economy. The chapter begins by noting that, although Russia has consistently allocated significant funds to its military, it faces economic difficulties that limit its spending capacity. With global sanctions in place, stemming from actions like the annexation of Crimea and involvement in Ukraine, Russia has had to make tough decisions about where to invest its resources. Despite these challenges, defense spending remains a top priority for the Russian government, reflecting the regime's belief in military strength as a means of asserting national power and influence.

The chapter further explores how Russia's military expenditures are allocated, with a focus on modernization efforts within its armed forces. From the development of new technologies like hypersonic missiles to the expansion of cyber capabilities, Russia has committed substantial funds to upgrading its military infrastructure. However, this focus on military strength has come at the expense of other sectors of the economy, such as healthcare, education, and social welfare. The author critiques this imbalance, noting that while Russia's defense spending bolsters its international standing, it does so at the cost of domestic well-being, leading to internal dissatisfaction and inequality.

Finally, the chapter reflects on the broader economic impact of Russia's defense spending. While the Russian economy has shown resilience in certain sectors, including energy exports, the overemphasis on military expenditures creates an unsustainable model. By dedicating a disproportionate amount of national wealth to defense, Russia may jeopardize its long-term economic stability. The chapter concludes by raising questions about how Russia will navigate this tension between military ambitions and the need for a more diversified and sustainable economy in the coming years.

12

Challenges in Modern Warfare

C hapter 11:

This chapter focuses on the evolving nature of warfare and how Russia is adapting to these challenges. It begins by addressing the shift from traditional warfare to hybrid and unconventional methods, such as cyberattacks, disinformation campaigns, and the use of proxy forces. Russia has been at the forefront of utilizing these tactics, which allow it to exert influence without direct military engagement. The chapter highlights instances like the alleged Russian interference in the 2016 U.S. presidential election and ongoing cyberattacks on critical infrastructure in the West, illustrating how Russia has embraced the concept of "asymmetric warfare" to challenge more powerful adversaries.

In addition to hybrid warfare, the chapter discusses how technological advancements are reshaping military operations. Russia's focus on developing advanced weaponry, such as AI-driven systems, drones, and advanced missile technologies, is a direct response to these new challenges. The chapter analyzes how these technologies are changing the landscape of combat, offering Russia a technological edge that allows it to compete with superior Western forces. At the same time, the chapter addresses the vulnerabilities of relying too heavily on technology, including the risks of cyber warfare and potential disruptions to Russia's own military infrastructure.

The chapter concludes by looking at the future of warfare, acknowledging that the landscape is continually evolving with new threats emerging. Russia's ability to adapt to these changes will be crucial in maintaining its military power and global influence. However, as the nature of warfare becomes more complex, Russia will need to balance its military advancements with efforts to safeguard against new forms of attack. The chapter emphasizes that Russia's future success in warfare will depend on its capacity to innovate while managing the risks posed by increasingly sophisticated adversaries.

13

The Future of Russian Military Power

C hapter 12:

This chapter speculates on the future of Russian military power and
the role it will play in global security. It begins by examining the
technological and strategic trends that will define Russia's military capabilities
in the coming decades. One of the key themes is the continued modernization
of Russia's armed forces, with a particular focus on the development of
autonomous systems, cyber warfare capabilities, and advanced weaponry.
The author predicts that Russia will continue to focus on these areas to
maintain a competitive edge over the West, especially as new global security
challenges emerge.

The chapter also looks at the political and economic factors that will shape Russia's military future. The ongoing conflict in Ukraine, relations with NATO, and the impact of international sanctions will all influence how Russia plans its military trajectory. The chapter highlights the importance of domestic stability and economic resilience in ensuring that Russia can sustain its military ambitions without risking economic collapse. The author suggests that Russia's future military strategy will be heavily influenced by its need to maintain a balance between military power and economic survival.

Finally, the chapter discusses the broader implications of Russia's military future for global security. As Russia continues to evolve its military strategy, it is likely to play a more assertive role in global conflicts, particularly in regions where it can exploit geopolitical vulnerabilities. The chapter concludes by acknowledging that while Russia's military power will remain formidable, its future success will depend on its ability to navigate a complex and unpredictable global environment, where new alliances, technological advancements, and shifting political landscapes will continuously reshape the international security order.

14

Book Conclusion

I n conclusion, Russia's military strength is deeply rooted in its historical achievements and its ability to adapt to the ever-changing global landscape. While its past victories and strategic positioning have played a crucial role in shaping its current status, the country's military force is constantly evolving in response to new technological advancements and shifting geopolitical dynamics. This evolution is not static; Russia is always seeking ways to refine its strategies, enhance its defense capabilities, and maintain its global influence. Whether it's through the modernization of its weapons systems, the incorporation of cyber warfare tactics, or the strengthening of its alliances, Russia's military continues to be a formidable force on the world stage.

Moreover, Russia's approach to military power is deeply intertwined with its national identity and its role in global politics. The country's military doctrine reflects a blend of pragmatism and ambition, aiming to assert dominance while navigating complex international relations. The evolution of its military force is not just about advancing technology or increasing firepower but also about making calculated moves in a broader geopolitical game. Russia's military posture remains a critical element in shaping its interactions with other nations, and understanding this dynamic is essential to grasping the intricacies of international diplomacy and power struggles.

As the world's geopolitical landscape continues to evolve, Russia's military dominance will remain a key factor in maintaining the balance of power. Its strategies and capabilities will continue to adapt to emerging threats, whether from traditional military conflicts or new arenas like cyber warfare and information battles. To fully understand the global balance, one must recognize Russia's ever-changing role in the world's power structure. The ongoing transformation of its military capabilities ensures that Russia will remain an essential player in global security, influencing the course of international relations for years to come.

www.ingramcontent.com/pod-product-compliance
Ingram Content Group UK Ltd.
Pitfield, Milton Keynes, MK11 3LW, UK
UKHW021839060225
454761UK00018B/569